How to Raise and Train an
ENGLISH
SPRINGER
SPANIEL

by Robert Gannon

Distributed in the U.S.A. by T.F.H. Publications, Inc., 211 West Sylvania Avenue, P.O. Box 27, Neptune City, N.J. 07753; in England by T.F.H. (Gt. Britain) Ltd., 13 Nutley Lane, Reigate, Surrey; in Canada to the book store and library trade by Clarke, Irwin & Company, Clarwin House, 791 St. Clair Avenue West, Toronto 10, Ontario; in Canada to the pet trade by Rolf C. Hagen Ltd., 3225 Sartelon Street, Montreal 382, Quebec; in Southeast Asia by Y.W. Ong, 9 Lorong 36 Geylang, Singapore 14; in Australia and the south Pacific by Pet Imports Pty. Ltd., P.O. Box 149, Brookvale 2100, N.S.W., Australia. Published by T.F.H. Publications, Inc. Ltd., The British Crown Colony of Hong Kong.

Photos by THREE LIONS, INC., New York, with the
cooperation of the author.

ISBN 0-87666-398-6

Contents

Above: As a hunter, a companion or a watchdog, the English Springer is unsurpassed He is a perfect all-round pet, for the breed is smart as well as gentle and sturdy.

Below: The ancestry of Springer Spaniels goes back to the Middle Ages and, in fact, some of these dogs came to Plymouth on the *Mayflower*. The dog pictured here with his master is not only a champion, but an aristocrat as well.

1. History of the Breed

Like a sailboat tacking into the wind, a dog zigzags across a dirt-brown cornfield. He covers the area with precision, working through every clump of foliage and scenting out pheasants enthusiastically, while his master shivers in the chill South Dakota dawn. With a startling whir of wings, a cock takes to the air. The dog sits as the hunter fires his gun. The pheasant is downed, wounded. On command, the dog takes off in pursuit, splashing over a swamp, rushing through still-standing corn and into a briar patch until, with a quick lunge, he grabs the bird and carries it proudly back to his master. A quick pat and a word of encouragement, and the dog sets out again.

This scene, duplicated across the United States at least a thousand times every fall, is typical of the teamwork of hunter and dog. The master could be anyone. The dog, likely as not, is an English Springer Spaniel.

Springers are hunters, and they're good. In fact, the majority of sporting men would agree that if a hunter has only one dog, he can't do better than to own an English Springer Spaniel. Why are these dogs so good in the field? They've been practicing for roughly a thousand years!

THE SPRINGER'S BACKGROUND

Some time during the early Middle Ages, according to most canine genealogists, a smart, strong, energetic and friendly dog migrated from Spain to France, then across the rest of Europe and the British Isles. Used for hunting small land animals and birds, the dog was called an "Espagnol" or, in English, "Spaniel," because of its origin.

In what was probably the first book to be written exclusively on hunting (between 1374 and 1377), Henri de Freeieres of France tells of the wonderful hunting ability and friendliness of this dog. Another writer-sportsman, Count Gaston de Foix, wrote of Spaniels in his *Livre de la Chasse* (*Book of the Chase*) of 1387:

> They love well their masters, follow them without losing them in crowds, and in fields go before them wagging their tails, and raise or start fowl for the falcons, and hares for the Greyhounds. When taught to crouch they are good to take partridge and quail with the net, and when taught to swim are also good for the river and for fowl that dive.

Before the day of the shotgun, birds and small animals were caught mainly by nets. It seems that wildlife was not so fearful of humans as it is today, for netting wasn't difficult at all. The hunter would let loose a trained hawk which, gliding across the sky, would frighten small birds and animals and cause them to hide. Then a Spaniel would sniff them out, crawl up to them as closely as possible and crouch down, allowing his master to throw a net over both dog and game. It is claimed that whole coveys of partridge could be netted in this way.

Later, hunters developed another technique. Using one of the larger Spaniels to crash through the underbrush and frighten the birds or animals into flight, they would set either a falcon or a Greyhound in pursuit of the game.

Gradually, the smaller dogs, trained to crouch and sneak up on game, became known as "Cocking Spaniels," or "Cock Flushers," since they were particularly adept at locating woodcock. These were the dogs we now call "Cockers." The larger dogs, used to "spring" game into the open, were called "Springing Spaniels" or, today, "Springers."

So successful at hunting were Spaniels, both large and small, that, oddly enough, their very skill made them unpopular with some French kings. Fearing that Spaniels would eliminate all game from the country, one king even outlawed the dogs.

Fortunately for the breed, however, everyone else loved them. Hunters applauded them for their first-class ability in the field. Ladies liked them because they were friendly and well-mannered in the parlor. The old and still current French proverb—"Love me, love my dog"—was based on the loyalty between Spaniel and master, and the dog was often mentioned in the works of early English writers. Shakespeare, for instance, in his "Henry VIII," wrote: *You play the Spaniel, /And think with wagging of your tongue to win me.*

For many centuries, Spaniels were called either "springing" or "cocking" merely because of their size and training, whether or not they came from the same litter. It wasn't until 1892, in fact, when the Kennel Club (England) gave Cocker Spaniels a separate classification, that they were finally recognized as a breed distinct from other Spaniels.

Springers, however, had to wait another decade before they bolstered sufficient strength and "fixity of type" to gain a show place of their own. Sir Hugo FitzHerbert deserves credit for publicizing Springers in England. With the help of a few other devotees, he exhibited his famous Tissington strain and won almost all prizes available.

Meanwhile, English Springers were gaining popularity in the New World. In fact, in spite of its name, the breed can be considered as American as any of us, for, according to Howard Chapin's "Dogs in Early New England," these Spaniels came to Plymouth on the first trip of the *Mayflower*.

Around 1866, sportsmen who lived in New Jersey and worked in New York are said to have made a practice of shooting for an hour or two with their Springers in the marshes of New Jersey before ferrying the Hudson River for a day of work.

The first English Springer Spaniel registered under that title in the American Kennel Club Stud Book was Denne Lucy (14264) in 1919, who was bred in England and imported to the United States by Hobart Ames of North Easton, Massachusetts.

The first Springer field trials in North America were held in Winnipeg, Canada, in September, 1922. One month later, seven Springers were exhibited at a show in Englewood, New Jersey. The English Springer Spaniel Field Trial Association, which held its first field trial on Fisher's Island, New York, was formed between 1924 and 1927, and became the breed's parent club.

Today's English Springer Spaniel, descendant of one of the oldest sporting dogs in the world (with, according to some, just a touch of Setter blood), ranks about twentieth in popularity among the 114 recognized breeds. The American Kennel Club lists something like 4,500 American Springers in its books.

THE DOG'S CHARACTERISTICS

Ask a Springer owner what's the best quality of his dog. Chances are he'll cite either hunting prowess or companionability, for Springers are outstanding in both these areas. Their affectionate, faithful dispositions make them especially tolerant of children—even the small tail-pulling variety. In addition, they are good guards, and possess an uncanny ability to discern between friend and foe. Above all, they're smart, a quality which you will appreciate in training them for the field or the home.

The best place to keep a Springer (and most other dogs, for that matter) is in the country. With plenty of nightly romping and long daytime walks, however, you can have a happy, healthy Springer even in the smallest mid-city apartment. The dog's fairly long hair keeps him warm in a backyard kennel, but he prefers

Springers are not at all irritable with children, even when treated roughly. Anyway, what dog wouldn't enjoy being surrounded by so many pals!

7

to spend most of his time with his master. Besides, his brain will develop faster and more fully if he is a companion rather than a possession.

An ungroomed dog will shed to a certain extent but, once he rids himself of his puppy coat, he will leave little hair on your furniture (that is, provided that you brush him properly—see pages 29-32).

Owners of Springers prefer them to Cockers for a couple of reasons. The dogs rarely show any of the nervousness occasionally seen in the smaller breed and, in the field, they have just enough more size and strength to be able to handle medium-size animals and the larger birds with ease.

All in all, when you own a well-trained English Springer Spaniel—whether he is a hunting companion, a show specimen or just a household friend—you have a dog whose intelligence, companionability and excellent disposition warrant your continuing pride.

STANDARDS OF THE BREED

The standards which have been adopted by the English Springer Spaniel Field Trial Association, and approved by the American Kennel Club, set the present-day ideal for which English Springer breeders are aiming. It is by these standards that the dog is judged in the show ring. However, even the most perfect specimen falls short of the standards in some respect. It's also impossible, even for a breeder or veterinarian, to tell how a puppy will shape up as an adult dog. The chances are that he will inherit the qualities for which his father and mother —or sire and dam in dog language—were bred, and if both his parents and grandparents had good show records he may have excellent possibilities.

Although they make cheerful, responsive pets, Springers are basically working dogs. Many sportsmen claim that this dog is the very finest breed for hunting.

Here, then, are the standards.

GENERAL APPEARANCE AND TYPE: The English Springer Spaniel is a medium-size sporting dog with a neat, compact body, and a docked tail. His coat is moderately long, glossy, usually liver and white or black and white, with feathering on his legs, ears, chest and brisket. His pendulous ears, soft gentle expression, sturdy build and friendly wagging tail proclaim him unmistakably a member of the ancient family of spaniels. He is above all a well proportioned dog, free from exaggeration, nicely balanced in every part. His carriage is proud and upstanding, body deep, legs strong and muscular with enough length to carry him with ease. His short level back, well developed thighs, good shoulders, excellent feet, suggest power, endurance, agility. Taken as a whole he looks the part of a dog that can go and keep going under difficult hunting conditions, and moreover, he enjoys what he is doing. At his best he is endowed with style, symmetry, balance, enthusiasm and is every inch a sporting dog of distinct spaniel character, combining beauty and utility. To be penalized: Those lacking true English Springer type in conformation, expression, or behavior.

TEMPERAMENT: The typical Springer is friendly, eager to please, quick to learn, willing to obey. In the show ring he should exhibit poise, attentiveness, tractability, and should permit himself to be examined by the judge without resentment or cringing. To be penalized: Excessive timidity, with due allowance for puppies and novice exhibits. But no dog to receive a ribbon if he behaves in vicious manner toward handler or judge. Aggressiveness toward other dogs in the ring *not* to be construed as viciousness.

SIZE AND PROPORTION: The Springer is built to cover rough ground with ability and reasonable speed. He should be kept to medium size—neither too small nor too large and heavy to do the work for which he is intended. The ideal shoulder height for dogs is 20 inches; for females, 19 inches. Length of topline (the distance from top or the shoulders to the root of the tail) should be approximately equal to the dog's shoulder height—never longer than his height—and not appreciably less. The dog too long in body, especially when long in loin, tires easily and lacks the compact outline characteristic of the breed. Equally undesirable is the dog too short in body for the length of his legs, a condition that destroys his balance and restricts the gait.

Weight is dependent on the dog's other dimensions: a 20-inch dog, well proportioned, in good condition should weigh about 49-55 pounds. The resulting appearance is a well-knit, sturdy dog with good but not too heavy bone, in no way coarse or ponderous. To be penalized: Over-heavy specimens, cloddy in build. Leggy individuals, too tall for their length and substance. Over-size or under-size specimens (those more than one inch under or over the breed ideal).

COLOR AND COAT: Color may be liver or black with white markings; liver and white (or black and white) with tan markings; blue or liver roan; or predominantly white with tan, black or liver markings. On ears, chest, legs and belly the Springer is nicely furnished with a fringe of feathering (of moderate heaviness). On his head, front or forelegs, and below hocks on front of hindlegs the hair is short and fine. The body coat is flat or wavy, of medium length, sufficiently dense to be water-proof, weather-proof and thorn-proof. The texture, fine and the hair should have the clean, glossy, live appearance indicative of good health. It is legitimate to trim about head, feet, ears; to remove dead hair; to thin and shorten excess feathering particularly from the hocks to the feet and elsewhere as required to give a smart, clean appearance. To be penalized: Rough, curly coat. Over-trimming especially of the body coat. Any chopped, barbered or artificial effect. Excessive feathering that destroys the clean outline desirable in a sporting dog. Off colors such as lemon, red or orange not to place.

HEAD: The head is impressive without being heavy. Its beauty lies in a combination of strength and refinement. It is important that the size and proportion be in balance with the rest of the dog. Viewed in profile the head should appear approximately the same length as the neck and should blend with the body in substance. The skull (upper head) to be of medium length, fairly broad, flat on top, slightly rounded at the sides and back. The occiput bone inconspicuous, rounded rather than peaked or angular. The foreface (head in front of the eyes) approximately the same length as the skull, and in harmony as to width and general character. Looking down on the head the muzzle to appear to be about one-half the width of the skull. As the skull rises from the foreface it makes a brow or "stop," divided by a groove or fluting between the eyes. This groove continues upward and gradually disappears as it reaches the middle of the forehead. The amount of "stop" can best be described as moderate. It must not be a pronounced feature as in the Clumber Spaniel. Rather it is a subtle rise where the muzzle blends into the upper head, further emphasized by the groove and by the position and shape of the eyebrows which should be well-developed. The stop, eyebrow and the chiseling of the bony structure around the eye sockets contribute to the Springer's beautiful and characteristic expression.

Viewed in profile the topline of the skull and the muzzle lie in two approximately parallel planes. The nasal bone should be straight, with no inclination downward toward the tip of the nose which gives a down-faced look so undesirable in this breed. Neither should the nasal bone be concave resulting in a "dish-faced" profile; nor convex giving the dog a Roman nose. The jaws to be of sufficient length to allow the dog to carry game easily; fairly square, lean, strong, and even (neither undershot nor overshot). The upper lip to come down full and rather square to cover the line of the lower jaw, but lips not to be pendulous nor exaggerated. The nostrils, well opened and broad, liver color or black depending on the color of the coat: Flesh-colored ("Dudley noses") or spotted ("butterfly noses") are undesirable. The cheeks to be flat (not rounded, full or thick) with nice chiseling under the eyes. To be penalized: Oval, pointed or heavy skull. Cheeks prominently rounded, thick and protruding. Too much or too little stop. Over heavy muzzle. Muzzle too short, too thin, too narrow. Pendulous slobbery lips. Under- or over-shot jaws—a very serious fault, to be heavily penalized. *Teeth*—The teeth should be strong, clean, not too small; and when the mouth is closed the teeth should meet in an even bite or a close scissors bite (the lower incisors touching the inside of the upper incisors). To be penalized: Any deviation from above description. One or two teeth slightly out of line not to be considered a serious fault, but irregularities due to faulty jaw formation to be severely penalized.

EYES: More than any other feature the eyes contribute to the Springer's appeal. Color, placement, size influence expression and attractiveness. The eyes to be of medium size, neither small, round, full and prominent, nor bold and hard in expression. Set rather well apart and fairly deep in their sockets. The color of the iris to harmonize with the color of the coat, preferably a good dark hazel in the liver dogs and black or deep brown in the black and white specimens. The expression to be alert, kindly, trusting. The lids, tight with little or no haw showing. To be penalized: Eyes yellow or brassy in color or noticeably lighter than the coat. Sharp expression indicating unfriendly or suspicious nature. Loose droopy lids. Prominent haw (the third eyelid or membrane in the inside corner of the eye).

EARS: The correct ear set is on a level with the line of the eye; on the side of the skull and not too far back. The flaps to be long and fairly wide, hanging close to the cheeks, with no tendency to stand up or out. The leather, thin, approximately long enough to reach the tip of the nose. To be penalized: Short round ears. Ears set too high or too low or too far back on the head.

NECK: The neck to be moderately long, muscular, slightly arched at the crest gradually blending into sloping shoulders. Not noticeably upright nor coming into the body at an abrupt angle. To be penalized: Short neck, often the sequence to steep shoulders. Concave neck, sometimes called ewe neck or upside down neck (the opposite of arched). Excessive throatiness.

BODY: The body to be well coupled, strong, compact; the chest deep but not so wide or round as to interfere with the action of the front legs; the brisket sufficiently developed to reach to the level of the elbows. The ribs fairly long, springing gradually to the middle of the body, then tapering as they approach the end of the ribbed section. The back (section between the withers and loin) to be straight and strong, with no tendency to dip or roach. The loins to be strong, short; a slight arch over loins and hip bones. Hips nicely rounded, blending smoothly into hind legs. The resulting topline slopes *very gently* from withers to tail—the line from withers to back descending without a sharp drop; the back practically level; arch over hips somewhat lower than the withers; croup sloping gently to base of tail; tail carried to follow the natural line of the body. The bottom line, starting on a level with the elbows, to continue backward with almost no up-curve until reaching the end of the ribbed section, then a more noticeable up-curve to the flank, but not enough to make the dog appear small waisted or "tucked up." To be penalized: Body too shallow, indicating lack of brisket. Ribs too flat sometimes due to immaturity. Ribs too round (barrel-shaped), hampering the gait. Sway-back (dip in back), indicating weakness or lack of muscular development, particularly to be seen when dog is in action and viewed from the side. Roach back (too much arch over loin and extending forward into middle section). Croup falling away too sharply; or croup too high —unsightly faults, detrimental to outline and good movement. Topline sloping sharply, indicating steep withers (straight shoulder placement) and a too low tail-set.

11

TAIL: The Springer's tail is an index both to his temperament and his conformation. Merry tail action is characteristic. The proper set is somewhat low following the natural line of the croup. The carriage should be nearly horizontal, slightly elevated when dog is excited. Carried straight up is untypical of the breed. The tail should not be docked too short and should be well fringed with wavy feather. It is legitimate to shape and shorten the feathering but enough should be left to blend with the dog's other furnishings. To be penalized: Tail habitually upright. Tail set too high or too low. Clamped down tail (indicating timidity or undependable temperament, even less to be desired than the tail carried too gaily).

FOREQUARTERS: Efficient movement in front calls for proper shoulders. The blades sloping back to form an angle with the forearm of approximately 90 degrees which permits the dog to swing his forelegs forward in an easy manner. Shoulders (fairly close together at the tips) to lie flat and mold smoothly into the contour of the body. The forelegs to be straight with the same degree of size to the foot. The bone, strong, slightly flattened, not too heavy or round. The knee, straight, almost flat; the pasterns short, strong; elbows close to the body with free action from the shoulders. To be penalized: Shoulders set at a steep angle limiting the stride. Loaded shoulders (the blades standing out from the body by overdevelopment of the muscles). Loose elbows, crooked legs. Bone too light or too coarse and heavy. Weak pasterns that let down the feet at a pronounced angle.

HINDQUARTERS: The Springer should be shown in hard muscular condition, well developed in hips and thighs and the whole rear assembly should suggest strength and driving power. The hip joints to be set rather wide apart and the hips nicely rounded. The thighs broad and muscular; the stifle joint strong and moderately bent. The hock joint somewhat rounded, not small and sharp in contour, and moderately angulated. Leg from hock joint to foot pad, short and strong with good bone structure. When viewed from the rear the hocks to be parallel whether the dog is standing or in motion. To be penalized: Too little or too much angulation. Narrow, undeveloped thighs. Hocks too short or too long (a proportion of ⅓ the distance from hip joint to foot is ideal). Flabby muscles. Weakness of joints.

FEET: The feet to be round, or slightly oval, compact, well arched, medium size with thick pads, well feathered between the toes. Excess hair to be removed to show the natural shape and size of the foot. To be penalized: Thin, open or splayed feet (flat with spreading toes). Hare foot (long, rather narrow foot).

MOVEMENT: In judging the Springer there should be emphasis on proper movement which is the final test of a dog's conformation and soundness. Prerequisite to good movement is balance of the front and rear assemblies. The two must match in angulation and muscular development if the gait is to be smooth and effortless. Good shoulders laid back at an angle that permits a long stride are just as essential as the excellent rear quarters that provide the driving power. When viewed from the front the dog's legs should appear to swing forward in a free and easy manner, with no tendency for the feet to cross over or interfere with each other. Viewed from the rear the hocks should drive well under the body following on a line with the forelegs, the rear legs parallel, neither too widely nor too closely spaced. Seen from the side the Springer should exhibit a good, long forward stride, without high-stepping or wasted motion. To be penalized: Short choppy stride, mincing steps with up and down movement, hopping. Moving with forefeet wide, giving roll or swing to body. Weaving or crossing of fore or hind feet. Cowhocks—hocks turning in toward each other.

In judging the English Springer Spaniel the over-all picture is a primary consideration. It is urged that the judge look for type which includes general appearance, outline and temperament and also for soundness especially as seen when the dog is in motion. Inasmuch as the dog with a smooth easy gait must be reasonably sound and well balanced he is to be highly regarded in the show ring, however, not to the extent of forgiving him for not looking like an English Springer Spaniel. A quite untypical dog, leggy, foreign in head and expression, may move well. But he should not be placed over a good all-round specimen that has a minor fault in movement. It should be remembered that the English Springer Spaniel is first and foremost a sporting dog of the Spaniel family and he must look and behave and move in character.

Toddlers and pups are natural companions, especially when the pups are cuddly Springer Spaniels, hungry for hugs and pats. Remember, though, no matter how good-natured your dog, the youngsters should be taught to handle him gently.

2. Selecting Your English Springer Spaniel

How much you spend for your Springer should depend on the purpose for which you are buying him. If you are planning to show your dog, then you want a puppy with good bloodlines and the possibility of developing into a champion. This may cost several hundred dollars, and if you are not an expert on dogs, you should have an expert help you make your selection.

If you want your Springer to be solely a pet or companion or guard for children, you can acquire a good dog for considerably less money. The fact that his conformation may be a bit off and his ancestors weren't champions won't make him any less valuable for your purposes.

WHERE TO BUY YOUR DOG

If it is a show dog you're seeking, you'll probably do best by getting your puppy from a kennel that specializes in Springers or a private breeder who exhibits. If you have the chance to visit a dog show, the Springer exhibitors there may have puppies for sale or can direct you to a good source.

If you're not so concerned about bloodlines, you can probably find the Springer for you at a pet shop or the pet section of a department store. If you live far from any source, you can buy a Springer by mail. Several of the larger mail order houses are in the dog business, too, and most kennels will ship a dog to you with the guarantee that the puppy is purebred and healthy.

THE PUPPY'S PAPERS

If you are investing in a purebred dog, obtain the necessary papers from the seller, especially if you are planning to show or breed your dog. Usually the litter will have been registered with the American Kennel Club. This is necessary before the individual puppy can be registered. The breeder should provide you with an Application for Registration signed by the owner of the puppy's mother. Then you select a name for your dog (it must be 25 letters or less, and cannot duplicate the name of another dog of the breed, or be the name of a living person without his written permission). Enter the selected name on the form, fill in the blanks that make you the owner of record, and send it to the American Kennel Club, 221 Park Avenue S., New York 3, N.Y., with the required fee. In a few weeks if all is in order, you will receive the blue and white Certificate of Registration with your dog's stud book number.

14

Which to choose? It would be hard to turn your back on *any* of these little fellows. But don't worry; they're so appealing that all these Springer pups are sure to find good homes.

THE PEDIGREE

The pedigree of your dog is a tracing of his family tree. Often the breeder will have the pedigree of the dog's dam and sire and may make out a copy for you. Or you can write to the American Kennel Club once your dog has been registered and ask for a pedigree. The fee depends on how many generations back you want the pedigree traced. In addition to giving the immediate ancestors of your dog, the pedigree will show whether there are any champions or dogs that have won obedience degrees in his lineage. If you are planning selective breeding, the pedigree is also helpful to enable you to find other Springers that have the same general family background.

A HEALTHY PUPPY

The healthy puppy will be active, gay and alert, with bright, shiny eyes. He should not have running eyes or nose. If the puppy in which you are interested seems listless, it may be that he has just eaten and wants to sleep for a while. Come back for a second look in a few hours, to see if he is more active.

A 3-month-old pup should not be fat or too stocky, but should be just a little bit "leggy," the legs being straight and medium in weight. Beware, however, of a dog that is too weedy looking.

The eyes should be so brown that they appear nearly black. Ears of a Springer pup should be below the level of the eyes. It's best if his coat is something other than a solid color, and there should be no red. It should be shiny and flat.

A somewhat older Springer should show a wide, deep chest. His neck should be rather long. In general, the dog should give the appearance of squareness. Avoid one that looks over-long. If you get a chance, study the dog's parents to see if they measure up to the Standards given on pages 8-13.

In buying a puppy—especially a higher-priced one—it is always wise to make your purchase subject to the approval of a veterinarian. The seller will usually allow you 8 hours in which to take the puppy to a vet to have his health checked. However, come to a clear agreement on what happens if the vet rejects the puppy. It should be understood whether rejection means that you get your money back or merely choice of another puppy from the same litter.

MALE OR FEMALE?

Unless you want to breed your pet and raise a litter of puppies it doesn't matter whether you choose a male or female. Both sexes are pretty much the same in disposition and character, and both make equally good pets. The male may be a bit more inclined to roam; the female is more of a homebody. A female's daily walks needn't be as long as the male's.

If you choose a female but decide you don't want to raise puppies, your dog can be spayed and will remain a healthy, lively pet.

No matter how irresistible he is, you should have a pup's physical condition checked by a veterinarian before you buy him. Make sure, too, that you and the seller have a clear understanding of what will happen if the dog is rejected.

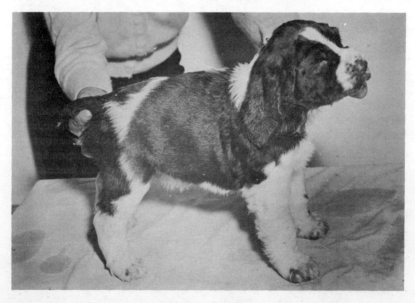

A well-built Springer pup should be slightly square in outline, as are the sturdy dogs pictured here. Straight, medium-weight legs are also characteristic of good dogs.

ADULT OR PUP?

Whether to buy a grown dog or a small puppy is another question. It is undeniably fun to watch your dog grow all the way from a baby, sprawling and playful, to a mature, dignified dog. If you don't have the time to spend on the more frequent meals, housebreaking, and other training a puppy needs in order to become a dog you can be proud of, then choose an older, partly trained pup or a grown dog. If you want a show dog, remember that no one, not even an expert, can predict with 100 per cent accuracy what a small puppy will be when he grows up.

WORMING AND INOCULATION

Before you take your puppy home find out from the breeder if he has already been wormed or inoculated for distemper and rabies. Practically all puppies will have worms which they acquire from eating worm eggs, from fleas, or from their mother. The breeder usually gives the puppies a worming before he sells them. If yours has already been wormed, find out when and what treatment was given. The breeder may be able to advise you on any further treatment that is necessary. While there are many commercial worming preparations on the market, it's generally safer to let the vet handle it. There will be more about worms in Chapter 3.

If your puppy has been inoculated against distemper, you will also have to know when this was done so you can give the information to your vet. He will complete the series of shots. If your puppy has not yet been given this protection, your vet should take care of it immediately. Distemper is highly prevalent and contagious. Don't let your puppy out of doors until he has had his distemper shots and they have had time to take effect.

As a rule, kennels and breeders do not inoculate puppies against rabies. In some areas, rabies inoculation is required by law. However, the possibility of your dog becoming affected with rabies, a contact disease, is very slight in most parts of the country. To be perfectly safe, check with your vet who will be familiar with the local ordinances and will advise you.

While the distemper inoculation is permanent and can be supplemented by "booster" shots, rabies inoculation must be repeated yearly. When your puppy receives it, the vet will give you a tag for the dog's collar certifying that he has received the protection. He will also give you a certificate for your own records. For foreign travel and some interstate travel, rabies inoculation is required.

The affectionate Springer just can't resist kissing his favorite people!

3. Caring for Your English Springer Spaniel

BRINGING YOUR PUPPY HOME

When you bring your puppy home, remember that he is used to the peace and relative calm of a life of sleeping, eating and playing with his brothers and sisters. The trip away from all this is an adventure in itself, and so is adapting to a new home. So let him take it easy for a while. Don't let the whole neighborhood pat and poke him at one time. Be particularly careful when children want to handle him, for they cannot understand the difference between the delicate living puppy and the toy dog they play with and maul. Show them the correct way to hold the puppy, supporting his belly with one hand while holding him securely with the other.

THE PUPPY'S BED

It is up to you to decide where the puppy will sleep. He should have his own place, and not be allowed to climb all over the furniture. He should sleep out of drafts, but not right next to the heat, which would make him too sensitive to the cold when he goes outside.

You might partition off a section of a room—the kitchen is good because it's usually warm and he'll have some companionship there. Set up some sort of low partition that he can't climb, give him a pillow or old blanket for his bed and cover the floor with a thick layer of newspapers. If he seems a bit timid or retiring, get a sturdy cardboard box, cut a large door in one side and put his bed in there.

You have already decided where the puppy will sleep before you bring him home. Let him stay there, or in the corner he will soon learn is "his," most of the time, so that he will gain a sense of security from the familiar. Give the puppy a little food when he arrives, but don't worry if he isn't hungry at first. He will soon develop an appetite when he grows accustomed to his surroundings. The first night the puppy may cry a bit from lonesomeness, but if he has an old blanket or rug to curl up in he will be cozy. In winter a hot water bottle will help replace the warmth of his littermates, or the ticking of a clock may provide company.

FEEDING THE PUPPY

By the time a puppy is 8 weeks old, he should be fully weaned and eating from a dish. Always find out what the seller has been feeding the puppy as it is well to keep him on the same diet for a while. Any sudden change in a puppy's feeding habits may cause loose bowels or constipation.

The following feeding schedule has been used on many Springers with good results.

Two Months Old

Morning: 5 or 6 tablespoons of milk (if cow's milk upsets your puppy, use half evaporated milk and half water), 3 or 4 tablespoons of baby cereal.

Noon: 1 or 2 heaping tablespoons of raw, finely ground meat or good quality canned dog food.

Afternoon: repeat the morning feeding.

Evening: repeat the noon feeding.

Before retiring: 5 or 6 tablespoons of milk.

Twice a day, give the puppy 1 or 2 teaspoons of cod liver oil, and your vet may suggest adding bone meal to one feeding.

Three Months Old

As the puppy's appetite increases, make his portions larger. When you begin housebreaking him, eliminate the late evening liquid and give him some dry food.

For the first few months, puppies need three meals a day and regular doses of cod liver oil. Eventually, at eight or ten months, the noon feeding can be omitted.

Give your new Springer his own bed as soon as you bring him home. He should sleep away from drafts, of course, but not too close to a radiator or hot air register. Like babies, puppies require intelligent, tender care.

FOUR-SIX MONTHS OLD

Morning: 1 cup of milk with 6 tablespoons of cereal or dog meal.

Noon: 4 to 8 heaping tablespoons of meat or dog meal.

Evening: repeat noon meal, adding about 5 tablespoons of cooked, mashed vegetables. Most vegetables are good.

Increase cod liver oil to 5 teaspoons twice a day.

SIX-EIGHT MONTHS OLD

Morning: 1½ cups of milk with 1½ cups of cereal or dog meal.

Noon: 1 cup of meat mixed with 1 cup of cereal.

Evening: 2 cups of meat, 1 cup of cereal, 1 cup of vegetables.

During the seventh month, gradually eliminate the noon meal.

EIGHT-TEN MONTHS OLD

Morning: 1½ cups of milk with 3 or 4 slices lightly buttered toast broken into it, or 8 tablespoons of cereal or dog meal.

Evening: 2 cups of meat, ½ cup of cereal or dog meal, 1 cup of vegetables (table scraps can be used).

Add 1½ tablespoons of cod liver oil twice a day to the diet, or use liquid or powdered vitamin supplement in food.

TEN-TWELVE MONTHS OLD

Morning: 1½ cups of milk with 3 slices toast or ½ cup cereal or dog meal.

Evening: 2 cups of meat, 1 cup cereal or meal, 1 cup vegetables.

Give 3 tablespoons of cod liver oil twice a day, or the amount of vitamin concentrate suggested on the label for adult dogs.

Reduce his main feeding to once daily, preferably in the late afternoon. His morning snack can be a few dog biscuits, a piece of toast, boiled egg or a share of your own breakfast menu. The main meal should consist of 2 cups of meat, 1 cup of cereal, toast or dog meal, 1½ cups of vegetables. During the colder months continue giving him cod liver oil and feed vitamin extract all year.

ADDITIONAL FEEDING TIPS

Occasional diarrhea in puppies may come from a change in food; if it persists, see your veterinarian.

Raw meat is considered better than cooked, but if your dog is ill, you should cook his meat. In any case, the food should be served at room temperature, never hot or cold.

As to the kind of meat, the lower-priced ground beef is preferable to the more expensive leaner cuts, since it contains a lot of fat that your dog needs in his diet. All kinds of liver, kidney, brains, and so forth are good. Of course you won't let your dog near chicken bones or fish with bones that can catch in his throat or tear his intestines. It is usually best not to feed him pork, fried meats or over-spiced foods.

Cream and cottage cheese are relished by most dogs and are nutritious. In addition, cottage cheese may stop mild diarrhea.

Green and yellow vegetables, cooked, are desirable dog foods, but some dogs react unfavorably to peas, onions and garlic. Cooked or raw fruit may be given, and while authorities agree that dogs do not need the Vitamin C in citrus foods, an occasional piece of orange or grapefruit may please your dog.

If you buy canned dog food, study the label carefully and make certain that it contains a large proportion of meat. The lower-priced foods are frequently overloaded with cereal and are low in protein content. If you feed dried food, add beef fat or bacon drippings.

To be absolutely sure that your dog is getting all the food values that he needs, you may want to buy a diet supplement for him. There are several preparations with all the necessary vitamins and minerals in one formula.

When your dog is fully grown he should be weighed every month. Never allow him to grow over 55 pounds. If he starts to get close to this weight, step up his daily exercise and cut down on his diet. Springers are hearty eaters—sometimes too hearty for their own good. A day or two without food won't harm a healthy dog. Many kennels "starve" their dogs one day a week, claiming that this keeps them more active and alert.

WATCHING THE PUPPY'S HEALTH

The first step in protecting the health of your puppy is a visit to the veterinarian. If the breeder has not given your puppy his first distemper shots, have your vet do it. You should also have your dog protected against hepatitis, and, if required by local law or if your vet suggests it, against rabies. Your puppy should receive his full quota of protective inoculations, especially if you plan to show him later. Select a veterinarian you feel you can trust and keep his phone number handy. Any vet will be glad to give a regular "patient" advice over the phone—often without charge. Occasional loose bowels in a puppy generally isn't anything too serious. It can be the result of an upset stomach or a slight cold. Sometimes it will clear up in a day or so without any treatment. If you want to help the puppy's digestion, add some cottage cheese to his diet, or, give him a few drops of kaopectate. Instead of tap water, give him barley or oatmeal water (just as you would a human baby). However, if the looseness persists for more than a day or two, a visit to the vet may be required. If the puppy has normal bowel movements alternating with loose bowel movements, it may be a symptom of worms.

If the puppy upchucks a meal or vomits up slime or white froth, it may indicate that his stomach is upset. One good stomach-settler is a pinch of baking soda, or about 8 or 10 drops of pure witch hazel in a teaspoon of cold water two or three times a day. In case of vomiting you should skip a few meals to give the stomach a chance to clear itself out. When you start to feed him again, give him cooked scraped beef for his first meals and then return to his normal diet. Persistent vomiting may indicate a serious stomach upset or even poisoning and calls for professional help.

WORMING

Practically all puppies start out life with worms in their insides, either acquired from the mother or picked up in their sleeping quarters. However, there are six different types of worms. Some will be visible in the stool as small white objects; others require microscopic examination of the stool for identification. While there are many commercial worm remedies on the market, it is safest to leave that to your veterinarian, and to follow his instructions on feeding the puppy before and after the worming. If you find that you must administer a worm remedy yourself, read the directions carefully and administer the smallest possible dose. Keep the puppy confined after treatment for worms, since many of the remedies have a strong laxative action and the puppy will soil the house if allowed to roam freely.

THE USEFUL THERMOMETER

Almost every serious puppy ailment shows itself by an increase in the puppy's body temperature. If your Springer acts lifeless, looks dull-eyed and gives an impression of illness, check by using a rectal thermometer. Hold the dog, insert the thermometer which has been lubricated with vaseline and take a reading. The normal temperature is 100.6 to 101.5 (higher than the normal human temperature). Excitement may send it up slightly, but any rise of more than a few points is cause for alarm.

SOME CANINE DISEASES

Your Springer is one of the sturdier breeds, not prone to many ailments which affect other dogs. Amateur diagnosis is dangerous because the symptoms of so many dog diseases are alike, but you should be familiar with some of the more prevalent ones which can strike your dog.

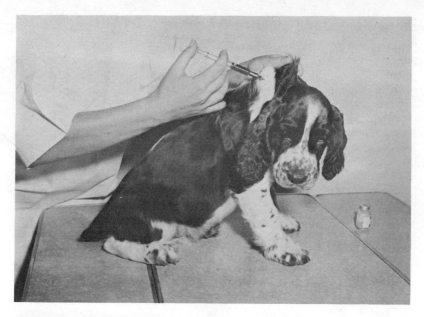

Above: Puppy health begins with a trip to the vet. Of the several important inoculations, distemper shots are the most crucial.

Below: The long, floppy ears of Spaniels require special attention. From time to time, clean out visible wax with a cotton swab moistened in boric acid solution.

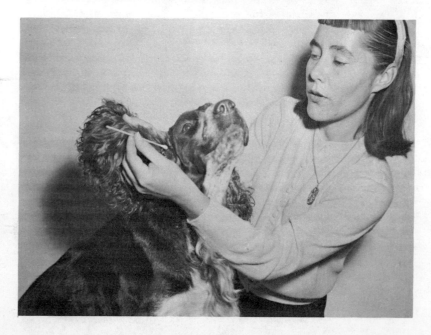

COUGHS, COLDS, BRONCHITIS, PNEUMONIA

Respiratory diseases may affect the dog because he is forced to live in a human rather than a natural doggy environment. Being subjected to a draft or cold after a bath, sleeping near an air conditioner or in the path of air from a fan or near a hot air register or radiator can cause one of these respiratory ailments. The symptoms are similar to those in humans. However, the germs of these diseases are different and do not affect both dogs and humans so that they cannot catch them from each other. Treatment is pretty much the same as for a child with the same illness. Keep the puppy warm, quiet, well fed. Your veterinarian has antibiotics and other remedies to help the pup fight back.

If your puppy gets wet, dry him immediately to guard against chilling. Wipe his stomach after he has walked through damp grass. Don't make the common mistake of running your dog to the vet every time he sneezes. If he seems to have a light cold, give him about a quarter of an aspirin tablet and see that he doesn't overexercise.

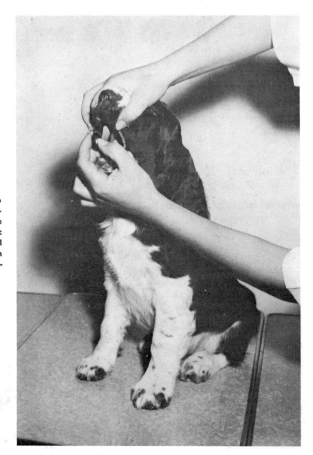

If your Springer pup has to "take his medicine," this is the proper way to give it to him. Once the pill is in, hold his mouth closed until he swallows it.

MAJOR DISEASES OF THE DOG

With the proper series of inoculations, your Springer will be almost completely protected against the following canine diseases. However, it occasionally happens that the shot doesn't take and sometimes a different form of the virus appears against which your dog may not be protected.

Rabies: This is an acute disease of the dog's central nervous system and is spread by the bite of an infected animal, the saliva carrying the infection. Rabies occurs in two forms. The first is "Furious Rabies" in which the dog shows a period of melancholy or depression, then irritation, and finally paralysis. The first period lasts from a few hours to several days. During this time the dog is cross and will try to hide from members of the family. He appears restless and will change his position often. He loses his appetite for food and begins to lick, bite and swallow foreign objects. During the "irritation" phase the dog is spasmodically wild and has impulses to run away. He acts in a fearless manner and runs and bites at everything in sight. If he is caged or confined he will fight at the bars, often breaking teeth or fracturing his jaw. His bark becomes a peculiar howl. In the final or paralysis stage, the animal's lower jaw becomes paralyzed and hangs down; he walks with a stagger and saliva drips from his mouth. Within four to eight days after the onset of paralysis, the dog dies.

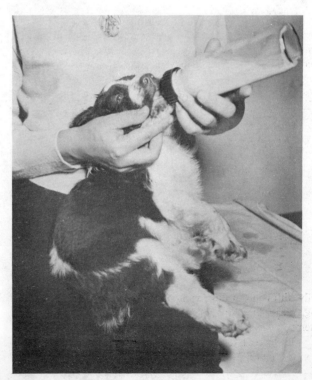

Bottle-feeding is seldom necessary. But if your pup loses his mother, is unusually weak or sick, you can feed him this way—just as you would a human baby.

The second form of rabies, "Dumb Rabies," is characterized by the dog's walking in a bear-like manner with his head down. The lower jaw is paralyzed and the dog is unable to bite. Outwardly it may seem as though he has a bone caught in his throat

Even if your pet should be bitten by a rabid dog or other animal, he can probably be saved if you get him to the vet in time for a series of injections. However, by the time the symptoms appear the disease is so far advanced that no cure is possible. But remember that an annual rabies inoculation is almost certain protection against rabies.

Distemper: Young dogs are most susceptible to distemper, although it may affect dogs of all ages. The dog will lose his appetite, seem depressed, chilled, and run a fever. Often he will have a watery discharge from his eyes and nose. Unless treated promptly, the disease goes into advanced stages with infections of the lungs, intestines and nervous system, and dogs that recover may be left with some impairment such as a twitch or other nervous mannerism. The best protection against this is very early inoculation—preferably even before the puppy is old enough to go out into the street and meet other dogs.

Hepatitis: Veterinarians report an increase in the spread of this virus disease in recent years, usually with younger dogs as the victims. The initial symptoms— drowsiness, vomiting, great thirst, loss of appetite and a high temperature— closely resemble distemper. These symptoms are often accompanied by swellings on the head, neck and lower parts of the belly. The disease strikes quickly and death may occur in a few hours. Protection is afforded by injection with a new vaccine.

Leptospirosis: This disease is caused by bacteria which live in stagnant or slow-moving water. It is carried by rats and dogs, and many dogs are believed to get it from licking the urine or feces of infected rats. The symptoms are increased thirst, depression and weakness. In the acute stage, there is vomiting, diarrhea and a brown discoloration of the jaws, tongue and teeth, caused by an inflammation of the kidneys. This disease can be cured if caught in time, but it is best to ward it off with a vaccine which your vet can administer along with the distemper shots.

External Parasites: The dog that is groomed regularly and provided with clean sleeping quarters should not be troubled with fleas, ticks or lice. However, it would be a wise precaution to spray his sleeping quarters occasionally with an anti-parasite powder that you can get at your pet shop or from your vet. If the dog is out of doors during the tick season he should be treated with a dip-bath.

Skin Ailments: Any persistent scratching may indicate an irritation, and whenever you groom your dog, look for the reddish spots that may indicate eczema or some rash or fungus infection. Rather than self-treatment, take him to the veterinarian as some of the conditions may be difficult to eradicate and can cause permanent harm to his coat.

FIRST AID FOR YOUR DOG

In general, a dog will lick his cuts and wounds and they'll heal. If he swallows anything harmful, chances are he'll throw it up. But it will probably make you feel better to help him if he's hurt, so treat his wounds as you would your own. Wash out the dirt and apply an antiseptic or ointment. If you put on a bandage, you'll have to do something to keep the dog from trying to remove it. A large cardboard ruff around his neck will prevent him from licking his chest or body. You can tape up his nails to keep him from scratching, or make a "bootie" for his paws.

If you think your dog has a broken bone, before moving him apply a splint just as you would to a person's limb. If there is bleeding that won't stop, apply a tourniquet between the wound and heart, but loosen it every few minutes to prevent damage to the circulatory system.

If you are afraid that your dog has swallowed poison and you can't get the vet fast enough, try to induce vomiting by giving him a strong solution of salt water or mustard in water.

SOME "BUTS"

First, don't be frightened by the number of diseases a dog can get. The majority of dogs never get any of them. If you need assurance, look at any book on human diseases. How many have you had?

Don't become a dog-hypochondriac. Veterinarians have enough work taking care of sick dogs and doing preventive work with their patients. Don't rush your pet to the vet every time he sneezes or seems tired. All dogs have days on which they feel lazy and want to lie around doing nothing.

THE FEMALE PUPPY

If you want to spay your female you can have it done while she is still a puppy. Her first seasonal period will probably occur between 8 and 10 months, although it may be as early as 6 or delayed until she is a year old. She may be spayed before or after this, or you may breed her (at a later season) and still spay her afterward.

The first sign of the female's being in season is a thin red discharge, which will increase for about a week, when it changes color to a thin yellowish stain, lasting about another week. Simultaneously there is a swelling of the vulva, the dog's external sexual organ. The second week is the crucial period, when she could be bred if you wanted her to have puppies, but it is possible for the period to be shorter or longer, so it is best not to take unnecessary risks at any time. After a third week the swelling decreases and the period is over for about six months.

If you have an absolutely climb-proof and dig-proof run within your yard, it will be safe to leave her there, but otherwise the female in season should be shut indoors. Don't leave her out alone for even a minute; she should be exercised only on leash. If you want to prevent the neighborhood dogs from hanging around your doorstep, as they inevitably will as soon as they discover that your female is in season, take her some distance away from the house before you let her relieve herself. Take her in the car to a nearby park or field for a chance to stretch her legs. After the three weeks are up you can let her out as before, with no worry that she can have puppies until the next season. But if you want to have her spayed, consult your veterinarian about the time and age at which he prefers to do it. With a young dog the operation is simple and after a night or two at the animal hospital she can be at home, wearing only a small bandage as a souvenir.

PROFESSIONAL GROOMING FOR YOUR SPRINGER

When your puppy reaches the age of 8 months he should begin to lose his puppy coat. At the time he starts shedding, you should help him along by manual grooming.

The grooming of a Springer is not done with an electric clipping machine. True, it is much faster and easier that way, but the quality of the job is obviously inferior. (If your Springer has been ignored for some time, his coat might be so matted and tangled that it is absolutely necessary to use an electric clipper. It must be assumed that you have been combing and brushing his coat periodically, thus insuring that his coat is in proper condition for grooming.)

It is so difficult to groom a Springer properly that you must have instruction om a professional. Consult your local Springer breeder for his advice.

BATHING AND BRUSHING YOUR SPRINGER

During the warm summer months you can give your pet a wet bath. Use any one of the many fine dog shampoos which are available at your pet supplier. Get a shampoo that will clean, deodorize and kill fleas all in one shot. Do not

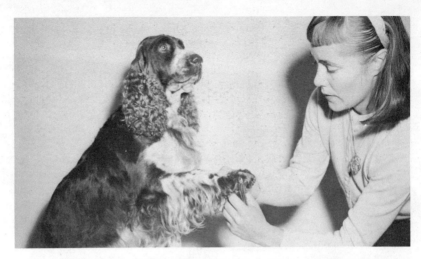

Shown above is a dog receiving a pedicure with clippers. But unless you're an expert and have learned from your vet how to use clippers without cutting blood vessels, it's safest to file your dog's nails.

Left: To weigh your pup, first get on the scales holding him, as shown here. Then, get off and weigh yourself. Subtract the second weight from the first— of course, the difference is the weight of the dog.

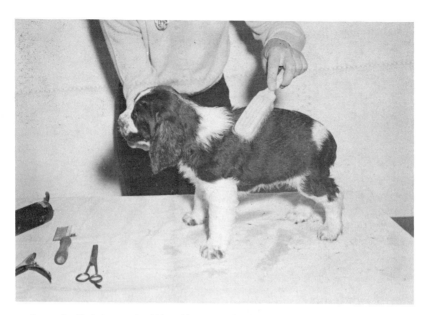

Even a tiny Springer pup should have his own comb and brush. His curly coat requires daily attention to prevent tangling.

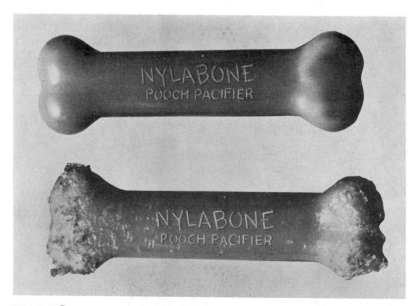

NYLABONE® is a necessity that is available at your local petshop (not in supermarkets). The puppy or grown dog chews the hambone flavored nylon into a frilly dog toothbrush, massaging his gums and cleaning his teeth as he plays. Veterinarians highly recommend this product . . . but beware of cheap imitations which might splinter or break.

expect to buy a fine shampoo at a cheap price. You will use it only a few times a year, and it pays off in dividends if you do the job properly.

During cold weather you can use one of the many dry baths available. In either case—whether you use a wet or a dry bath—bathe your Springer frequently. Otherwise, like all Spaniels, he will develop an odor.

To keep your Springer looking his very best, it's wise to buy your puppy his own comb and brush. Use the brush as often as possible . . . every day if you can. It will not only give your dog a healthier coat, but it will make bathing and clipping that much easier. A Springer whose long coat is full of knots must have a clip quite close to the skin or he will not look at all the way a proper Springer should look.

Use the comb to take out knots and tangles, but be humane about it and work the knots out very slowly.

WATCH THE TOENAILS

Many dogs that run on gravel or pavements keep their toenails down, so they seldom need clipping. But a dog that doesn't do much running, or runs on grass, will grow long toenails that can be harmful. The long nails will force the dog's toes into the air and spread his feet wide. In addition, the nails may force the dog into an unnatural stance that may produce lameness.

You can control your dog's toenails by cutting them with a special dog clipper or by filing them. Many dogs object to the clipping and it takes some experience to learn just how to do it without cutting into the blood vessels. Your vet will probably examine your dog's nails whenever you bring him in and will trim them at no extra charge. He can show you how to do it yourself in the future. If you prefer, you can file the points off your dog's nails every few weeks with a flat wooden file. Draw the file in only one direction—from the top of the nail downward in a round stroke to the end of the nail or underneath. You'll need considerable pressure for the first few strokes to break through the hard, polished surface, but then it gets easier.

Incidentally, it's a good idea to keep your young puppy from walking on waxed or slippery floors, as this tends to break down the pasterns.

EYES, EARS AND TEETH

If you notice matter collecting in the corners of the dog's eyes, wipe it out with a piece of cotton or tissue. If there is a discharge, check with your vet.

The Springer's ears should receive daily care. Brush the ear flap to remove any matted dirt or food. Examine the ears and remove all visible wax, using a piece of cotton dipped in a boric acid solution or a solution of equal parts of water and hydrogen peroxide. Be gentle and don't probe into the ear, but just clean the parts you can see. If your dog constantly shakes his head, twitches his ears or scratches them, it is best to have the vet take a look.

If you give your dog a hard chewing bone—the kind you can buy at a pet store—it will serve him as your toothbrush serves you and will prevent the accumulation of tartar on his teeth. However, check his mouth occasionally and take him to the vet if you find collected tartar or bloody spots on his gums.

Once he has been trained, even a tot can manage a well-disciplined Springer. Intelligence, combined with amiability, makes this breed ideal for almost any family, but particularly for those which include small children and sportsmen. With this dog, it's impossible to go wrong.

4. Housebreaking and Training Your English Springer Spaniel

The first months of your puppy's life will be a busy time. While he's getting his preventive shots and becoming acquainted with his new family, he should learn the elements of housebreaking that will make him a welcome addition to your home and community.

HOUSEBREAKING THE PUPPY

Housebreaking the puppy isn't difficult because his natural instinct is to keep the place where he sleeps and plays clean. The most important factor is to keep him confined to a fairly small area during the training period. You will find it almost impossible to housebreak a puppy who is given free run of the house. After months of yelling and screaming, you may finally get it through his head that the parlor rug is "verboten," but it will be a long, arduous process.

FIRST, PAPER TRAINING

Spread papers over the puppy's living area. Then watch him carefully. When you notice him starting to whimper, sniff the ground or run around in agitated little circles, rush him to the place that you want to serve as his "toilet" and hold him there till he does his business. Then praise him lavishly. When you remove the soiled papers, leave a small damp piece so that the puppy's sense of smell will lead him back there next time. If he makes a mistake, wash it immediately with warm water, followed by a rinse with water and vinegar. That will kill the odor and prevent discoloration.

It shouldn't take more than a few days for the puppy to get the idea of using newspaper. When he becomes fairly consistent, reduce the area of paper to a few sheets in a corner. As soon as you think he has the idea fixed in his mind, you can let him roam around the house a bit, but keep an eye on him. It might be best to keep him on leash the first few days so you can rush him back to his paper at any signs of an approaching accident.

The normally healthy puppy will want to relieve himself when he wakes up in the morning, after each feeding and after strenuous exercise. During early puppyhood any excitement, such as the return home of a member of the family or the approach of a visitor, may result in floor-wetting, but that phase should pass in a few weeks.

OUTDOOR HOUSEBREAKING

Keep in mind during the housebreaking process that you can't expect too much from your puppy until he is about 5 months old. Before that, his muscles and digestive system just aren't under his control. However, you can begin outdoor training even while you are paper training the puppy. (He should have learned to walk on lead at this point. See page 44.) First thing in the morning, take him outdoors (to the curb if you are in a city) and walk him back and forth in a small area until he relieves himself. He will probably make a puddle and then just walk around uncertain of what is expected of him. You can try standing him over a piece of newspaper which may give him the idea. Some dog trainers use glycerine suppositories at this point for fast action. Praise the dog every time taking him outside brings results and he'll get the idea. After each meal take him to the same spot.

Use some training word to help your puppy learn. Pick a word that you won't use for any other command and repeat it while you are walking your dog in his outdoor "business" area. It will be a big help when the dog is older if you have some word of command that he can connect with approval to relieve himself in a strange place. You'll find, when you begin the outdoor training, that the male puppy usually requires a longer walk than the female. Both male and female puppies will squat. It isn't until he's quite a bit older that the male dog will begin to lift his leg.

NIGHTTIME TRAINING

If you hate to give up any sleep, you can train your Springer puppy to go outdoors during the day and use the paper at night for the first few months. After he's older, he'll be able to contain himself all night and wait for his first morning walk. However, if you want to speed up the outdoor training so that you can leave the dog alone in the house with less fear of an accident, keep him confined at night so that he has enough room to move around in his bed but not enough to get any distance away from it. When he has to go, he'll whine loudly enough to attract your attention. Then take him or let him out. You may have to get up once or twice a night for a few weeks but then you can be fairly sure that your puppy will behave indoors—although accidents will happen. Sometimes even a grown dog will suddenly—and for no apparent reason—soil the house, usually the most expensive carpet in it.

Occasionally a puppy that seems to have been housebroken will revert to indiscriminate acts all over the place. If that happens it may be necessary to go back to the beginning and repeat the paper training.

WHEN HE MISBEHAVES

Rubbing a puppy's nose in his dirt or whacking him with a newspaper may make you feel better, but it won't help train the puppy. A dog naturally *wants* to do the right thing for his master. Your job is to show him what you want. If an accident happens, ignore it unless you can catch him immediately and then in a firm tone express your displeasure and take him to the spot he should have used. A puppy has a short memory span, and bawling him out for some-

The Springer's head-line combines strength with grace. Ideally, the upper head is rather broad, flat at the top and a bit rounded at the sides and back. The muzzle blends subtly into the upper head.

thing that happened a half-hour before will have no meaning to him. When he does use the right place, be lavish with praise and petting, but first be sure he has finished. Many a puppy has left a trail of water across a floor because someone interrupted him to tell him how well he was doing.

PUPPY DISCIPLINE

A 6- or 8-week-old puppy is old enough to understand what is probably the most important word in his vocabulary—"NO!" The first time you see the puppy doing something he shouldn't do, chewing something he shouldn't chew or wandering in a forbidden area, it's time to teach him. Shout "No" and stamp your foot, hit the table with a piece of newspaper or make some other loud noise. Dogs, especially very young ones, don't like loud noises and your misbehaving pet will readily connect the word with something unpleasant. If he persists, repeat the "No," hold him firmly and slap him sharply across the nose. Before you protest to the A.S.P.C.A. you should realize that a dog does not resent being disciplined if he is doing something wrong and is caught in the act. However, do not chase a puppy around while waving a rolled-up newspaper at him or trying to swat him. Punish him only when you have a firm hold on him. Above all, never call him to you and then punish him. He must learn to associate coming to you with something pleasant.

If the comical Maltese Terrier shown here is a stranger in the house, his Springer Spaniel
companions don't seem to be aware of it. They're just good pals, as are the members of the
sleepy trio pictured below.

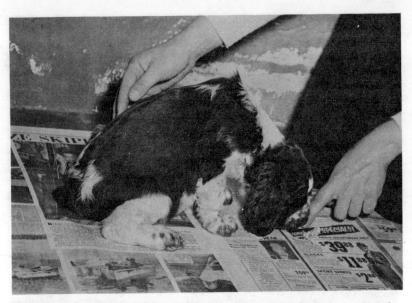

Above: Paper training is every pup's first lesson in good manners. If you leave a scrap of damp paper when you throw out the soiled ones, your pup will have no trouble performing in the right place next time.

Below: A firm "No" when your pup settles down for a snooze on the sofa will help him learn that his place is on the floor. Everybody loves a plush seat, but the floor is the place for pets.

Above: "Maybe when I wake up, I'll feel more like playing." Like children, pups should have toys of their own. A hard rubber bone is an excellent choice.

Below: Training not only makes your dog easy to live with, it also protects him from accidents. Of course, it's crucial to teach your dog to stay far away from moving cars. A firm "No" is always the best training aid.

The alert Springer is easily trained, both for obedience and field work. Once you discover how responsive your dog is, you may want to enter him in American Kennel Club obedience trials. Dogs which cannot take part in regular breed shows and spayed females are eligible to compete for obedience titles.

Daily ear care is a necessity for your Springer Spaniel. His ears should be brushed to keep them free from dirt and food, and excess wax should be removed whenever necessary to prevent infections and parasites.

Every puppy will pick things up. So the second command should be "Drop it!" or "Let go!" Don't engage in a tug-of-war with the puppy, but take the forbidden object from him even if you have to pry his jaws open with your fingers. Many dogs will release what they are holding if you just blow sharply into their faces. Let your dog know that you are displeased when he picks up something he shouldn't.

If you give him toys of his own, he will be less liable to chew your possessions. Avoid soft rubber toys that he can chew to pieces. Don't give him cloth toys, either, as he'll probably swallow pieces and have trouble getting them out of his system. Skip the temptation to give him an old slipper, because it will be hard for him to distinguish between that and a brand-new pair you certainly won't want him to chew. Your pet shop will have some indestructible toys that will be fine for your Springer.

However, even with training, reconcile yourself to the fact that during puppy-hood things will be chewed and damaged, but that's a passing phase in the growth of a dog.

JUMPING ON PEOPLE

Your friendly Springer will like people, and the puppy may try to show his affection by jumping and climbing all over you and everyone else he likes. You may think this is cute while he's still a puppy, but it's a habit you have to break. If you're planning to show him, you won't want him climbing all over the judge in the ring. Besides, not all your friends and relatives are dog lovers and many people prefer to admire dogs from a slight distance. One way to cure the jumping habit is to lift your knee and send him flying back. Ask your friends to respond to his too-friendly greeting this way too. Another method is to grab the dog's front paws and flip him backward, or you can try stepping on his hind paws. Soon he'll develop a more restrained greeting. But he should be patted afterward so he won't think people are hostile.

And here's a tip on petting the puppy. If everyone pets him on top of the head, as most people do, he may develop the habit of coming over to people with his head down to receive his due. Instead, he should be chucked under the chin. That will keep him in an attractive head-up pose when he greets people—and improve his posture in the show ring or on the street.

CLIMBING ON FURNITURE

If your Springer shows a fondness for climbing on furniture, this is another habit you'll have to break early. The upholstery holds the scent of the people he likes, and besides, it's more comfortable than the hard floor or even the carpet. Sometimes verbal corrections will be enough to establish the fact that the furniture is taboo. If not, try putting crinkly cellophane on the furniture to keep him off. If that doesn't work, you can get liquids at your pet store that you can't smell, but whose odor keeps the dog off.

Once your puppy has mastered the essentials of living with people, he is ready to learn all the other things that will make him welcome in the neighborhood. Further training is discussed in the next chapter.

5. Obedience Training for Your English Springer Spaniel

The purpose of obedience training is not to turn your dog into a puppet but to make him a civilized member of the community in which he will live, and to keep him safe. This training is most important as it makes the difference between having an undisciplined animal in the house or having an enjoyable companion. Both you and your dog will learn a lot from training.

HOW A DOG LEARNS

The dog is the one domestic animal that seems to want to do what his master asks. Unlike other animals that learn by fear or rewards, the dog will work willingly if he is given a kind word or a show of affection.

The hardest part of dog training is communication. If you can get across to the dog what you want him to do, he'll do it. Always remember that your dog does not understand the English language. He can, however, interpret your tone of voice and your gestures. By associating certain words with the act that accompanies them, the dog can acquire a fairly large working vocabulary. Keep in mind that it is the sound rather than the meaning of the words that the dog understands. When he doesn't respond properly, let him know by the tone of your voice that you are disappointed, but follow each correction with a show of affection.

YOUR PART IN TRAINING

You must patiently demonstrate to your dog what each simple word of command means. Guide him with your hands and the training leash through whatever routine you are teaching him. Repeat the word associated with the act. Demonstrate again and again to give the dog the chance to make the connection in his mind. (In psychological language, you are conditioning him to give a specific response to a specific stimulus.)

Once he begins to get the idea, use the word of command without any physical guidance. Drill him. When he makes mistakes, correct him, kindly at first, more severely as his training progresses. Try not to lose your patience or become irritated, and never slap him with your hand or the leash during a training session. Withholding praise or rebuking him will make him feel badly enough.

When he does what you want, praise him lavishly with words and with pats. Don't rely on dog candy or treats in training. The dog that gets into the habit of performing for treats will seldom be fully dependable when he can't smell or see one in the offing. When he carries out a command, even though his performance is slow or sloppy, praise him and he will perform more readily the next time.

THE TRAINING VOICE

When you start training your Springer, use your training voice, giving commands in a firm, clear tone. Once you give the command, persist until it is obeyed even if you have to pull the dog protestingly to obey you. He must learn that training is different from playing, that a command once given must be obeyed no matter what distractions are present. Remember that the tone and sound of your voice, not loudness, are the qualities that will influence your dog.

Be consistent in the use of words during training. Confine your commands to as few words as possible and never change them. It is best for only one person to carry on the dog's training because different people will use different words and tactics that will confuse the animal. The dog who hears "come," "get over here," "hurry up," "here, Rover," and other commands when he is wanted will become totally confused.

TAKE IT EASY

Training is hard on the dog—and on the trainer. A young dog just cannot take more than 10 minutes of training at a stretch, so limit the length of your first lessons. You'll find that you too, will tend to become impatient when you stretch out a training session, and losing your temper won't help either of you. Before and after each lesson have a play period, but don't play during a training session. Even the youngest dog soon learns that schooling is a serious matter; fun comes afterward.

Don't spend too much time on one phase of training or the dog will become bored. And always try to end a training session on a pleasant note. If the dog doesn't seem to be getting what you are trying to show him, go back to something simpler that he can do. This way you will end every lesson with a pleasant feeling of accomplishment. Actually, in nine cases out of ten, if your dog isn't doing what you want, it's because you're not getting the idea over to him properly.

WALKING ON LEAD

"Doggy" people call the leash a "lead," so we'll use that term here. With your Springer, don't go in for any kind of fancy lead or collar. The best lead for training purposes is the 6-foot webbed-cloth lead, usually olive-drab in color.

As for the collar, you'll need a metal-link collar called a "choke" collar. Even though the name may sound frightening, it won't hurt your dog and it's an absolute *must* in training. It tightens when you snap the lead, eases when you relax your grip. It's important to put the collar on properly. Slide the chain around your dog's neck so that you can attach the lead to the ring at the end of the chain which passes *over*, not under, his neck.

Put the collar and lead on the puppy and let him walk around the house first with the lead dragging on the floor. This is just to let him get the feel of

Start training early, but keep each session short—not more than 10 minutes each at first. The pup shown here is being taught to walk on a lead. His trainer correctly holds the lead in her right hand.

the strange object around his neck. But a word of caution for afterward: don't let the dog wander around with the choke collar on. If it's loose he'll lose it, and it's possible for it to catch on any projection and choke him. For his license tag and rabies tag you can get a light leather collar that fits more snugly.

Now, here's a lesson for you. From the start, hold the lead firmly in your right hand. Keep the dog at your left side. You can use your left hand to jerk the lead when necessary to give corrections or to bring the dog closer to you. Do not *pull* on the lead. Give it a sharp snap when you want to correct the dog, and then release it. The dog cannot learn from being pulled around. He will learn when he finds that doing certain things results in a sharp jerk; doing other things allows him to walk comfortably on lead.

At first, the puppy will fight the lead. He'll probably plant all four feet or his rear end on the ground and wait for your next move. Be patient. Short tugs on the lead will help him learn his part in walking with you. If he gets overexcited, calm him before taking off the lead and collar and picking him up. He must learn there's nothing to fear. (Incidentally, if the lesson is being given on a city street, it might be a good idea to carry some paper to clean up the mess he may leave in his excitement.)

TRAINING TO SIT

Training your dog to sit should be fairly easy. Stand him on your left side, holding the lead fairly short, and command him to "Sit." As you give the verbal command, pull up slightly with the lead and push his hindquarters down (you may have to kneel to do this). Do not let him lie down or stand up. Keep him in a sitting position for a moment, then release the pressure on the lead and praise him. Constantly repeat the command word as you hold him in a sitting position, thus fitting the word to the action in his mind. After a while, he will begin to get the idea and will sit without your having to push his back down. When he reaches that stage, insist that he sit on command. If he is slow to obey, slap his hindquarters with the end of the lead to get him down fast. Teach him to sit on command facing you as well as when he is at your side. When he begins sitting on command with the lead on, try it with the lead off.

THE "LIE DOWN"

The object of this is to get the dog to lie down either on the verbal command "Down!" or when you give him a hand signal, your hand raised, palm toward the dog—a sort of threatening gesture. This is one of the most important parts of training. A well-trained dog will drop on command and stay down whatever the temptation—car-chasing, cat-chasing, or another dog across the street.

Don't start this until the dog is almost letter-perfect in sitting on command. Then, place the dog in a sit. Force him down by pulling his front feet out forward while pressing on his shoulders and repeating "Down!" Hold the dog down and stroke him gently to let him know that staying down is what you expect of him.

After he begins to get the idea, slide the lead under your left foot and give the command "Down!" At the same time, pull on the lead. This will help get the dog down. Meanwhile, raise your hand in the down signal. Don't expect to accomplish all this in one session. Be patient and work with the dog. He'll cooperate if you show him just what you expect him to do.

THE "STAY"

The next step is to train your dog to stay in either a "sit" or "down" position. Sit him at your side. Give him the command "Stay," but be careful not to use his name with that command as hearing his name may lead him to think that some action is expected of him. If he begins to move, repeat "Stay" firmly and hold him down in the sit. Constantly repeat the word "Stay" to fix the meaning of that command in his mind. When he stays for a short time, gradually increase the length of his stay. The hand signal for "Stay" is a downward sweep of your hand toward the dog's nose, with the palm toward him. While he is sitting, walk around him and stand in front of him. Hold the lead at first; later, drop the lead on the ground in front of him and keep him sitting. If he bolts, correct him severely and force him back to a sit in the same place.

Use some word such as "okay" or "up" to let him know when he can get up, and praise him well for a good performance. As this practice continues, walk farther and farther away from him. Later, try sitting him, giving him the command to stay, and then walk out of sight, first for a few seconds, then for longer periods. A well-trained dog should stay where you put him without moving for three minutes or more.

Similarly, practice having him stay in down position, first with you near him, later when you step out of sight.

THE "COME" ON COMMAND

A young puppy will come a-running to people, but an older puppy or dog will have other plans of his own when his master calls him. However, you can train your dog to come when you call him if you begin when he is young. At first, work with him on lead. Sit the dog, then back away the length of the lead and call him, putting as much coaxing affection in your voice as possible. Give an easy tug on the lead to get him started. When he does come, make a big fuss over him and it might help to hand him a piece of dog candy or food as a reward. He should get the idea soon. Then attach a long piece of cord to the lead—15 or 20 feet—and make him come to you from that distance. When he's coming pretty consistently, have him sit when he reaches you.

Don't be too eager to practice coming on command off lead. Wait till you are certain that you have the dog under perfect control before you try calling him when he's free. Once he gets the idea that he can disobey a command to come and get away with it, your training program will suffer a serious setback. Keep in mind that your dog's life may depend on his immediate response to a command to come when he is called. If he disobeys off lead, put the collar back on and correct him severely with jerks of the lead. He'll get the idea.

In training your dog to come, never use the command when you want to punish him. He should associate the "Come" with something pleasant. If he comes very slowly, you can speed his response by pulling on the lead, calling him and running backward with him at a brisk pace.

At first, practice the "sit," "down," "stay" and "come" indoors; then try it in an outdoor area where there are distractions to show the dog that he must obey under any conditions.

HEELING

"Heeling" in dog language means having your pet walk alongside you on your left side, close to your left leg, on lead or off. With patience and effort you can train your dog to walk with you even on a crowded street or in the presence of other dogs. However, don't begin this part of his training too early. Normally, a dog much under 6 months old is just too young to absorb the idea of heeling.

Put the dog at your left side, sitting. Then say "Heel" firmly and start walking at a brisk pace. Do not pull the dog with you, but guide him by tugs at the lead. Keep some slack on the lead and use your left hand to snap the lead for a correction. Always start off with your left foot and after a while the dog will learn to watch that foot and follow it. Keep repeating "Heel" as you walk, snapping the dog back into position if he lags behind or forges ahead. If he gets out of control, reverse your course sharply and snap him along after you. Keep up a running conversation with your dog, telling him what a good fellow he is when he is heeling, letting him know when he is not.

At first limit your heeling practice to about 5 minutes at a time; later extend it to 15 minutes or a half-hour. To keep your dog interested, vary the routine. Make right and left turns, change your pace from a normal walk to a fast trot to a very slow walk. Occasionally make a sharp about-face.

Having learned to "heel," or walk at your left side on or off the lead, your Springer should also sit in heel position when you stop walking. He shouldn't get up until you give another command to "Heel."

Remember to emphasize the word "Heel" throughout this practice and to use your voice to let him know that you are displeased when he goes ahead or drops behind or swings wide.

If you are handling him properly, the dog should begin to get the idea of heeling in about 15 minutes. If you get no response whatever, if the dog runs away from you, fights the lead, gets you and himself tangled in the lead, it may indicate that he is still young, or that you aren't showing him what you expect him to do.

Practicing 15 minutes a day, in 6 or 7 weeks your pet should have developed to the stage where you can remove the lead and he'll heel alongside you. First try throwing the lead over your shoulder or fastening it to your belt, or remove the lead and tie a piece of thin cord (fishing line will do nicely) to his collar. Then try him off lead. Keep his attention by constantly talking; slap your left leg to keep his attention on you. If he breaks away, return to the collar and lead treatment for a while.

"HEEL" MEANS SIT, TOO

To the dog, the command "Heel" will also mean that he has to sit in heel position at your left side when you stop walking—with no additional command from you. As you practice heeling, force him to sit whenever you stop, at first using the word "Sit," then switching over to the command "Heel." He'll soon get the idea and plop his rear end down when you stop and wait for you to give the command "Heel" and start walking again.

TEACHING TO COME TO HEEL

The object of this is for you to stand still, say "Heel!" and have your dog come right over to you and sit by your left knee in heel position. If your dog has been trained to sit without command every time you stop, he's ready for this step.

Sit him in front of and facing you and step back a few feet. Say "Heel" in your most commanding tone of voice and pull the dog into heel position, making him sit. There are several different ways to do this. You can swing the dog around behind you from your right side, behind your back and to heel position.

All dogs, but especially those who are to participate in breed shows, should master the "stand." Your dog should be able to stay still in one spot and permit a stranger to run his hands over his body without showing impatience or resentment.

Or you can pull him toward you, keep him on your left side and swing him to heel position. Use your left heel to straighten him out if he begins to sit behind you or crookedly. This may take a little work, but the dog will get the idea if you show him just what you want.

THE "STAND"

Your Springer should be trained to stand on one spot without moving his feet, and should allow a stranger to run his hands over his body and legs without showing any resentment or fear. Use the same method you used in training him to stay on the sit and down. While walking, place your left hand out, palm toward his nose, and command him to stay. His first impulse will be to sit, so be prepared to stop that by placing your hand under his body. If he's really stubborn, you may have to wrap the lead around his body near his hindquarters and hold him up until he gets the idea that this is different from the command to sit. Praise him for standing and walk to the end of the lead. Correct him strongly if he starts to move. Have a stranger approach him and run his hands over the dog's back and down his legs. Keep him standing until you come back to him. Walk around him from his left side, come to heel position, and let the dog sit as you praise him lavishly.

JUMPING EXERCISES

Most Springers love to jump, and it won't be hard to teach yours to jump over a hurdle at your command, then return to you. First let him approach the hurdle and examine it. Then go back about 10 feet and run toward it with the dog, holding the lead. When you reach it, shout "Over" or "Up" excitedly. Make a game of it. If the dog hesitates, it may be necessary for you to jump over it with him the first few times to give him confidence. After he jumps alone, call him and guide him back to you with the lead. After a while you can put him in sit position, facing the jump, say his name and give the command, and he will take the hurdle and return to sit in front of you. Oddly enough, a dog that is trained to jump on command will not develop the habit of jumping fences when left alone.

SIMPLE RETRIEVING

Whether or not you intend to use your Springer to retrieve, he should have some training in the occupation for which he was bred. It will be fun for you to teach him to fetch on command, and helpful to you when he has mastered his lessons. Use a wooden dumbbell, a thick dowel stick or a thin, rolled-up magazine. While you have the dog heeling on lead, hold the object in front of him and tease him by waving it in front of his nose. Then say "Take it" and let him grab it. Walk with him while he's carrying it, and then say "Give" and take it from his mouth. If he drops it first, pick it up and tease him until he takes it again and holds it until you remove it.

With the dog still on lead, throw the object a few feet in front of him and encourage him to pick it up and hold it. If he won't give it up when you want it, don't have a tug-of-war. Just blow into his nostrils and he'll release his hold. Then praise him as if he had given it to you willingly.

Don't expect to accomplish all the training overnight. Generally a dog-training school will devote about 10 weeks, with one session a week, to all this training. Between lessons the dogs and their masters are expected to work about 15 minutes every day on the exercises.

If you'd like more detailed information on training your dog, you'll find it in the pages of HOW TO HOUSEBREAK AND TRAIN YOUR DOG, a Sterling-T.F.H. book.

There are dog-training classes in all parts of the country, some sponsored by the local A.S.P.C.A. A free list of dog-training clubs and schools is available from the Gaines Dog Research Center, 250 Park Avenue, New York, New York.

If you feel that you lack the time or the skill to train your dog yourself, there are professional dog trainers who will do it for you, but basically dog training is a matter of training *you* and your dog to work together as a team, and if you don't do it yourself you will miss a lot of fun.

ADVANCED TRAINING AND OBEDIENCE TRIALS

Once you begin training your Springer and see how well he does, you'll probably be bitten by the "obedience bug"—the desire to enter him in obedience trials held under American Kennel Club license. Most dog shows now include obedience classes at which your dog can qualify for his "degrees" to demonstrate his usefulness as a companion dog, not merely as a pet or show dog.

The A.K.C. obedience trials are divided into three classes: Novice, Open and Utility.

The Springer is primarily used for retrieving upland birds. However, never use a wounded bird during training, but a dead one with its wings tied together.

In the "stand" position your dog should keep his head erect and high and his tail up. At first you may have to help him get the idea by lifting his tail slightly, as shown above.

In the Novice Class, the dog will be judged on the following basis:

Test	Maximum Score
Heel on leash	35
Stand for examination by judge	30
Heel free—off leash	45
Recall (come on command)	30
1-minute sit (handler in ring)	30
3-minute down (handler in ring)	30
Maximum total score	200

If the dog "qualifies" in three different shows by earning at least 50 per cent of the points for each test, with a total of at least 170 for the trial, he has earned the Companion Dog degree and the letters C.D. are entered in the stud book after his name.

After the dog has qualified as a C.D., he is eligible to enter the Open Class competition where he will be judged on this basis:

Test	Maximum Score
Heel free	40
Drop on recall	30
Retrieve (wooden dumbbell) on flat	25
Retrieve over obstacle (hurdle)	35
Broad jump	20
3-minute sit (handler out of ring)	25
5-minute down (handler out of ring)	25
Maximum total score	200

Springers just naturally love water. Even so, it's unwise to start your dog on swimming lessons until he's at least 10 months old. Premature heavy exercise may prevent the proper development of his legs.

Again he must qualify in three shows for the C.D.X. (Companion Dog Excellent) title and then is eligible for the Utility Class where he can earn the Utility Dog degree in these rugged tests:

Test	Maximum Score
Scent discrimination (picking up article handled by master from group of articles)—Article 1...............	20
Scent discrimination—Article 2.................................	20
Scent discrimination—Article 3.................................	20
Seek back (picking up article dropped by handler).........	30
Signal exercise (heeling, etc., on hand signal only).........	35
Directed jumping (over hurdle and bar jump)...............	40
Group examination...	35
Maximum total score...	200

For more complete information about these obedience trials, write to the American Kennel Club, 221 Park Avenue S., New York 3, N.Y., and ask for their free booklet "Regulations and Standards for Obedience Trials." Spayed females and dogs that are disqualified from breed shows because of physical defects (see the Standards in Chapter 1) are eligible to compete in these trials.

Besides the formal A.K.C. obedience trials, there are informal "match" shows in which dogs compete for ribbons and inexpensive trophies. These shows are run by local Springer clubs and by all-breed obedience clubs, and in many localities the A.S.P.C.A. and other groups conduct their own obedience shows. Your local pet shop or kennel can keep you informed about such shows in your vicinity and you will find them listed in the different dog magazines or in the pet column of your local paper.

FIELD TRAINING AND RETRIEVING

If you plan to hunt with your Springer, you should begin field training early. It will take months of patient training before the two of you can do a good job on a hunt, and sometimes years may pass before you develop into a really top-notch team. If you want a well-trained dog but haven't the time to devote to his schooling, send him to a professional trainer. Prices for boarding and training generally are standard across the United States. They may vary, of course, according to the degree of perfection you desire and the reputation of the trainer. Ordinarily, it takes about 6 weeks to break a fairly alert Springer if he receives once-a-day training by competent handlers.

The task of an English Springer is to find game—ordinarily, upland birds, but the breed can also be trained for ground animals—by ranging back and forth along the hunting course just ahead of the gunner. When the game is flushed and the bird is hit, the dog immediately sits until he is told to go after the bird, then finds it and returns it to his master.

Springers do not point. The Brittany is the only Spaniel that does, since this job is usually reserved for Pointers and Setters.

The first lesson in the field is fetching. Spaniels are born retrievers—they love to carry things—so this part of your dog's schooling will probably be easy. For field work, a training dummy is better than a ball. You can make one yourself from a stocking stuffed with excelsior, 3 inches in diameter and a foot long. A small, light, cork-filled boat bumper is also very good. Perhaps the best is an ordinary fielder's glove. This will sail through the air like a bird when you throw it and, with a little practice, you can place it wherever you want with accuracy.

Fling the dummy 20 feet or more and, when the dog picks it up, stoop down, clap your hands and call him by name. When he finally brings the dummy to you (this may take a number of trials), lavish praise on him. You have already taught him to sit on command, so make use of this when he approaches you with the dummy. Don't try to grab it from him or engage in a tug-of-war. If he won't give you the dummy, put your hand over his upper jaw and, with your fingers on one side, your thumb on the other, press his lips against his upper teeth. When the object falls to the ground, say "Drop," and praise him when he gives it to you willingly. Combine the sit with the drop, and soon he'll do the two things automatically.

Incidentally, if you start to lose your temper or if the dog begins to get contrary, call it a day. Remember that the whole training procedure should be fun for both you and the dog.

After your Springer learns to fetch, teach him to wait until you want him to retrieve. When you throw the dummy, say "Sit," instead of "Fetch," and hope that he'll obey you. Probably he won't. If he persists in running after the thrown object immediately, try using a 15-foot check cord. As he nears the end of the cord, yell "Sit!" After a few mid-air flips when he reaches the cord end, he'll learn that you mean it when you tell him to sit.

After the dog has mastered the initial retrieving lessons, get down to business with real field training. Don't train in the same place every day; move to new areas. In addition to two dummies, you will need a whistle and a revolver with blanks.

Now comes the quartering lesson, when you teach the dog to zigzag in order to cover the area ahead of you. First, select a distant object as your walking goal. Then, with the command "Go on," start walking at an angle from your general line of advance. Your pup will rush from you, eager to lead the way. After 15 yards or so, blow your whistle twice and turn, much as a sailboat might tack into the wind. Your pup will look around to see what all the noise is about. When he sees that you're walking in a new direction, he'll start to bound off with you. Wave him on with your hand. At first he won't notice it, but eventually he might, which is a big help in later training. Keep up this zigzagging, whistle-blowing and hand-waving for several lessons. Then gradually make your turn angle smaller and smaller until you're walking in a straight line, your Springer zigzagging ahead. Be sure to keep him within gun range.

When these lessons seem to be going well, start shooting off blanks every so often, accompanying the shots with the command to sit. Soon your dog will learn to sit whenever the gun goes off. Be sure to use good judgment when first introducing him to the sound of the gun. Fire it when he is some distance away. Some trainers recommend starting with a cap pistol to guard against frightening the dog.

Training a dog to be a first-rate hunter is a long job and one which requires great patience. But the results will make the effort well worth while. Incidentally, your Springer can be trained to retrieve ground animals as well as birds.

Now start integrating the retrieving with the gun-shooting, using more than one dummy to show the dog that there may be more than a single bird downed. Throw dummies or sail your fielder's gloves in opposite directions, and send your dog after the first one thrown. This ensures that he won't see where the second one lands. Guide him to the unseen dummy by a combination of whistle-blows and hand-waves. This training will probably require several lessons, but it is an essential part of a Spaniel's hunting education.

Perhaps the hardest thing to do is to teach a dog to keep going in a straight line; most just can't seem to grasp this concept. The best way to go about this is to start in reverse—send him back along your path.

As you walk along, drop the dummy where your dog can see it, but keep walking on ahead. Twenty feet or so further, turn around and say, "Go on," and the dog will, with luck, go back and fetch it. Do this a number of times (and for several days), gradually increasing the distance. Then, still allowing your Springer to see where the dummy is dropped, make a turn in your course before sending him back. Then walk in circles. Always when you send him, command him to go on, and accompany the command with an overhead throwing motion.

Then drop the dummy when the dog is looking the other way, and send him back for it. Finally, when he is accustomed to following directions, plant a dummy and return to it a few hours later. Send the dog on ahead to find it, using a combination of whistle-blows to change directions, and the command to go on with the overhand signal. To bring him back, teach him to return when you sound one long toot on your whistle.

Proceed slowly with water retrieving lessons. Don't pick the dog up and throw him into the water, but put on a bathing suit and get into it yourself. Make it fun, like a game, as the whole training process should be.

Incidentally, though Springers nearly always love water, hold off swimming instructions until your dog reaches 10 months. If a pup is allowed to do much early swimming, his legs might not develop properly.

FIELD TRIALS

Field trials give you an opportunity to test your Springer under actual hunting conditions against other English Springer Spaniels and other sporting breeds. At both the informal sanctioned field trials and the formal A.K.C. trials you will meet other people with your interest in dogs. The best source of information about these trials is the American Field Magazine, 222 West Adams Street, Chicago, 6, Illinois.

Make an effort to visit a field trial as a spectator, see the dogs and handlers in action and ask questions. You'll find the people friendly and ready to welcome you and your Springer into the fraternity of the Field.

6. Caring for the Female and Raising Puppies

Whether or not you bought your female dog intending to breed her, some preparation is necessary when and if you decide to take this step.

WHEN TO BREED

It is usually best to breed on the second or third season. Plan in advance the time of year which is best for you, taking into account where the puppies will be born and raised. You will keep them until they are at least 6 weeks old, and a litter of frisky pups takes up considerable space by then. Other considerations are selling the puppies (Christmas vs. springtime sales), your own vacation, and time available to care for them. You'll need at least an hour a day to feed and clean up after the mother and puppies but probably it will take you much longer—with time out to admire and play with them!

CHOOSING THE STUD

You can plan to breed your female about 6½ months after the start of her last season, although a variation of a month or two either way is not unusual. Choose the stud dog and make arrangements well in advance. If you are breeding for show stock, which may command better prices, a mate should be chosen with an eye to complementing the deficiencies of your female. If possible, they should have several ancestors in common within the last two or three generations, as such combinations generally "click" best. He should have a good show record or be the sire of show winners if old enough to be proven.

The owner of such a male usually charges a fee for the use of the dog. The fee varies. This does not guarantee a litter, but you generally have the right to breed your female again if she does not have puppies. In some cases the owner of the stud will agree to take a choice puppy in place of a stud fee. You should settle all details beforehand, including the possibility of a single surviving puppy, deciding the age at which he is to make his choice and take the pup, and so on.

If you want to raise a litter "just for the fun of it" and plan merely to make use of an available male Springer, the most important point is temperament. Make sure the dog is friendly as well as healthy, because a bad disposition could appear in his puppies, and this is the worst of all traits in a dog, destined to be a pet. In such cases a "stud fee puppy," not necessarily the choice of the litter, is the usual payment.

The English Springer Spaniel Field Trial Association, which is working to keep the quality of Springers at a high level, is a good source of information when you are looking for a mate for your dog. Many members have stud dogs available, and if you want to breed your female, it will be worth while to join the club. The American Kennel Club will give you, on request, the name and address of the Secretary of the English Springer Spaniel Field Trial Association.

PREPARATION FOR BREEDING

Before you breed your female, make sure she is in good health. She should be neither too thin nor too fat. Any skin disease *must* be cured, before it can be passed on to the puppies. If she has worms she should be wormed before being bred or within three weeks afterward. It is generally considered a good idea to revaccinate her against distemper and hepatitis before the puppies are born. This will increase the immunity the puppies receive during their early, most vulnerable period.

The female will probably be ready to breed 12 days after the first colored discharge. You can usually make arrangements to board her with the owner of the male for a few days, to insure her being there at the proper time, or you can take her to be mated and bring her home the same day. If she still appears receptive she may be bred again two days later. However, some females never show signs of willingness, so it helps to have the experience of a breeder. Usually the second day after the discharge changes color is the proper time, and she may be bred for about three days following. For an additional week or so she may have some discharge and attract other dogs by her odor, but can seldom be bred.

THE FEMALE IN WHELP

You can expect the puppies 9 weeks from the day of breeding, although 61 days is as common as 63. During this time the female should receive normal care and exercise. If she was overweight, don't increase her food at first; excess weight at whelping time is bad. If she is on the thin side build her up, giving her a morning meal of cereal and egg yolk. You may add one of the mineral and vitamin supplements to her food, to make sure that the puppies will be healthy. As her appetite increases, feed her more. During the last weeks the puppies grow enormously and she will probably have little room for food and less appetite. She should be tempted with meat, liver and milk, however.

As the female in whelp grows heavier, cut out violent exercise and jumping. Although a dog used to such activities will often play with the children or run around voluntarily, restrain her for her own sake. However, don't eliminate exercise entirely. Walking is very beneficial to the female in whelp, and a daily moderate walk will help her keep up her "muscle tone" in preparation for the birth.

PREPARING FOR THE PUPPIES

Prepare a whelping box a few days before the puppies are due, and allow the mother to sleep there overnight or to spend some time in it during the day to become accustomed to it. Then she is less likely to try to have her pups under the front porch or in the middle of your bed. The box should have a wooden floor. Sides about a foot high will keep the puppies in but enable the mother to get out after she has fed them. If the weather is cold, the box should be raised about an inch off the floor.

Layers of newspaper spread over the whole area will make excellent bedding and be absorbent enough to keep the surface warm and dry. They should be removed daily and replaced with another thick layer. An old quilt or washable blanket makes better footing for the nursing puppies than slippery newspaper during the first week, and is softer for the mother.

Be prepared for the actual whelping several days in advance. Usually the female will tear up papers, refuse food and generally act restless. These may be false alarms; the real test is her temperature, which will drop to below 100° about 12 hours before whelping. Take it with a rectal thermometer morning and evening, and put her in the pen, looking in on her frequently, when the temperature goes down.

WHELPING

Usually little help is needed, but it is wise to stay close to make sure that the mother's lack of experience does not cause an unnecessary accident. Be ready to help her when the first puppy arrives, for it could smother if she does not break the membrane enclosing it. She should start right away to lick the puppy, drying and stimulating it, but you can do it with a soft rough towel, instead. The afterbirth should follow the birth of each puppy, attached to the puppy by the long umbilical cord. Watch to make sure that each is expelled, anyway, for retaining this material can cause infection. In her instinct for cleanliness the mother will probably eat the afterbirth after biting the cord. One or two will not hurt her; they stimulate milk supply as well as labor for remaining pups. But too many can make her lose appetite for the food she needs to feed her pups and regain her strength. So remove the rest of them along with the wet newspapers and keep the pen dry and clean to relieve her anxiety.

If the mother does not bite the cord, or does it too close to the body, take over the job, to prevent an umbilical hernia. Tearing is recommended, but you can cut it, about two inches from the body, with a sawing motion of scissors, sterilized in alcohol. Then dip the end in a shallow dish of iodine; the cord will dry up and fall off in a few days.

The puppies should follow each other at intervals of not more than half an hour. If more time goes past and you are sure there are still pups to come, a brisk walk outside may start labor again. If she is actively straining without producing a puppy it may be presented backward, a so-called "breech" or upside down birth. Careful assistance with a well-soaped finger to feel for the puppy or ease it back may help, but never attempt to pull it by force against the mother.

RAISING THE PUPPIES

Hold each puppy to a breast as soon as he is dry, for a good meal without competition. Then he may join his littermates in the basket, out of his mother's way while she is whelping. Keep a supply of evaporated milk on hand for

If the mother seems a bit overwhelmed, it may be because nursing a large litter is a strain. Make sure the new mother gets large quantities of liquids, so that she can produce all the milk her pups need.

emergencies, or later weaning. A formula of evaporated milk, corn syrup and a little water with egg yolk should be warmed and fed in a doll or baby bottle if necessary. A supplementary feeding often helps weak pups over the hump. Keep track of birth weights and take weekly readings so you will have an accurate record of the pups' growth and health.

After the puppies have arrived, take the mother outside for a walk and drink, and then leave her to take care of them. She will probably not want to stay away more than a minute or two for the first few weeks. Be sure to keep water available at all times, and feed her milk or broth frequently, as she needs liquids to produce milk. To encourage her to eat offer her the foods she likes best, until she asks to be fed without your tempting her. She will soon develop a ravenous appetite and should have at least two large meals a day, with dry food available in addition.

Prepare a warm place to put the puppies after they are born to keep them dry and help them to a good start in life. Cover an electric heating pad or hot-water bottle with flannel and put it in the bottom of a cardboard box. Set the box near the mother so that she can see her puppies. She will usually allow you to help, but don't take the puppies out of sight, and let her handle things if your interference seems to make her nervous.

Be sure that all the puppies are getting enough to eat. If the mother sits or stands, instead of lying still to nurse, the probable cause is scratching from the puppies' nails. You can remedy this by clipping them, as you do hers. Manicure scissors will do for these tiny claws.

Some breeders advise disposing of the smaller or weaker pups in a large litter, as the mother has trouble in handling more than six or seven. But you can help her out by preparing an extra puppy box or basket. Leave half the litter with the mother and the other half in a warm place, changing off at two hour intervals at first. Later you may change them less frequently, leaving them all together except during the day. Try supplementary feeding, too; as soon as their eyes open, at about two weeks, they will lap from a dish, anyway.

The puppies should normally be completely weaned at five weeks, although you start to feed them at three weeks. They will find it easier to lap semi-solid food. At four weeks they will eat four meals a day, and soon do without their mother entirely. Start them on mixed dog food, or leave it with them in a dish for self-feeding. Don't leave water with them all the time; at this age everything is to play with and they will use it as a wading pool. They can drink all they need if it is offered several times a day, after meals.

As the puppies grow up the mother will go into the pen only to nurse them, first sitting up and then standing. To dry her up completely, keep the mother away for longer periods; after a few days of part-time nursing she can stay away for longer periods, and then completely. The little milk left will be reabsorbed.

AIRING THE PUPPIES

The puppies may be put outside, unless it is too cold, as soon as their eyes are open, and will benefit from the sunlight and vitamins. A rubber mat or newspapers underneath will protect them from cold or damp.

You can expect the pups to need at least one worming before they are ready to go to new homes, so take a stool sample to your veterinarian before they are three weeks old. If one puppy has worms all should be wormed. Follow the veterinarian's advice, and this applies also to vaccination. If you plan to keep a pup you will want to vaccinate him at the earliest age, so his littermates should be done at the same time.

7. Showing Your English Springer Spaniel

You probably think that your Springer is the best in the country and possibly in the world, but before you enter the highly competitive world of the show, get some unbiased expert opinions. Compare your dog against standards on pages 8-13. If a Springer club in your vicinity is holding a match show, enter your dog and see what the judges think of him. If he places in a few match shows, then you might begin seriously considering the big-time shows. Visit a few as a spectator first and make careful mental notes of what is required of the handlers and the dogs. Watch how the experienced handlers manage their dogs to bring out their best points. See how they use pieces of liver to "bait" the dogs and keep them alert in the ring. If experts think your dog has the qualities to make him a champion, you might want to hire a professional handler to show him.

HOW TO ENTER

If your dog is purebred and registered with the American Kennel Club—or eligible for registration—you may enter him in the appropriate show class for which his age, sex and previous show record qualify him. You will find coming shows listed in the different dog magazines. Write to the secretary of the show, asking for the "Premium List." When you receive the entry form, fill it in carefully and send it back with the required entry fee. Then, before the show, you'll receive your Exhibitor's Pass which will admit you and your dog to the show.

Here are the five official show classes:

Puppy Class: Open to dogs at least 6 months and not more than 12 months of age. Limited to dogs whelped in the United States and Canada.

Novice Class: Open to dogs 6 months of age or older that have never won a first prize at a show—wins in puppy class excepted. Limited to dogs whelped in the United States or Canada.

Bred by Exhibitor Class: Open to all dogs except champions 6 months of age or over who are exhibited by the same person or kennel that was the recognized breeder on the records of the American Kennel Club.

American-Bred Class: Open to dogs that are not champions, 6 months of age or over, whelped in the United States after a mating which took place in the United States.

Open Class: Open to dogs 6 months of age or over, with no exceptions. In addition there are local classes, "special classes" and brace entries.

For full information on the dog show rules, see *How to Show Your Own Dog*, by Virginia Tuck Nichols (T.F.H.).

ADVANCE PREPARATION

Before you go to a show your dog should be trained to gait at a trot beside you, with head up and in a straight line. In the ring you will have to gait around the edge with other dogs and then individually up and down the center runner. In addition the dog must stand for examination by the judge, who will look at him closely and feel his head and body structure. He should be taught to stand squarely, hind feet slightly back, head up on the alert. He must hold the pose when you place his feet and show animation for a piece of boiled liver in your hand or a toy mouse thrown in front of you.

Showing requires practice training sessions in advance. Get a friend to act as judge and set the dog up and "show" him for a few minutes every day.

If you have kept your Springer well groomed all along, he will need little special grooming for the show, just be sure he looks his best.

The day before the show, pack your kit. You will want to take a water dish and bottle of water for your dog (so that he won't be affected by a change in drinking water, and you won't have to go look for it). Take the show lead, the grooming tools and the identification ticket sent by the show superintendent, noting the time you must be there and the place where the show will be held, as well as the time of judging.

THE DAY OF THE SHOW

Don't feed your dog the morning of the show, or give him at most a light meal. He will be more comfortable in the car on the way, and will show more enthusiastically. When you arrive at the show grounds an official veterinarian will check your dog for health, and then you should find his bench and settle him there. Locate the ring where Springers will be judged, take the dog to the exercise ring to relieve himself, and give him a small drink of water. After a final grooming, you have only to wait until your class is called. It is your responsibility to be at the ring at the proper time.

Then, as you step into the ring, try to keep your knees from rattling too loudly. Before you realize it you'll be out again, perhaps back with the winners for more judging and finally—with luck—it will be all over and you'll have a ribbon and an armful of silver trophies. And a very wonderful dog!